RANDOM THOUGHTS

by
Howard (Howie) Fuchs

Leaning Rock Press
Gales Ferry, CT

Leaning Rock Press
Gales Ferry, CT 06335
leaningrockpress@gmail.com
www.leaningrockpress.com

978-1-960596-67-3, Hardcover
978-1-960596-68-0, Softcover

Library of Congress Control Number: 2025915744

Publisher's Cataloging-In-Publication Data
(Prepared by Cassidy Cataloguing's PCIP Service)

Names:	Fuchs, Howard, author.
Title:	Random thoughts / by Howard (Howie) Fuchs.
Description:	Gales Ferry, CT : Leaning Rock Press, [2025]
Identifiers:	LCCN: 2025915744 | ISBN: 9781960596673 (hardcover) | 9781960596680 (softcover)
Subjects:	LCSH: Families. | Parenting. | Emotions. | Courage. | Travel. | Life. | Wisdom. | BISAC: BODY, MIND & SPIRIT / Mindfulness & Meditation. | BODY, MIND & SPIRIT / New Thought. | SELF-HELP / Personal Growth / General.
Classification:	LCC: PS3606.U26 R36 2025 | DDC: 818/.6--dc23

Printed in the United States of America

DEDICATION

This Dedication is long because I have a huge family. To my Wife, Daughter, 3 adult Sons, 3 Daughters-in-law, 6 informally adopted Sons, Goddaughter, Godson and 5 gorgeous, brilliant, talented and funny Grandchildren. Now extended family: To my Brother, Brothers-in-law, Sisters-in-law, Nephews, Nieces, Cousins, Brothers from other Mothers and Sisters from other Mothers.

All of you have inspired me.

CONTENTS

INTRODUCTION 1

FAMILY and FRIENDS 2

PARENTING and KIDS 12

EMOTIONS 22

TRAVEL. 32

LIFE 40

RANDOM THOUGHTS 50

WISDOM Of OTHERS 74

SPECIAL ACKNOWLEGMENTS 83

INTRODUCTION

Since this is my first book I tried to keep it short, easy to read with broad based appeal. There is little fluff, filler or drawn out explanations. The book has a variety of thoughts from serious to educational to funny to obvious. It can be easily read at bedtime or during layovers in the Airport. Hopefully people of all ages will discover something that touches and inspires them.

FAMILY
and
FRIENDS

Happiness is a growing Family…
and Special Events or Holidays to celebrate it.

The best part of being in a close Family is the
opportunity to enjoy the uniqueness of your role and
the individual connections it offers you...
Son (Daughter), Brother (Sister),
Husband (Wife), Father (Mother),
Father-in-Law (Mother-in-Law),
Grandfather (Grandmother),
Uncle (Aunt)...
Each relationship enriches your life in its own special way.

Cruises with Immediate and Extended Family
is an excellent way to solidify the bonds…
Also, lots of fun!

Family offers great inspiration
to do new things,
like writing your first book.

Family is not only about those
who are born or marry into it…
but also, Friends who feel like Family…
"Brothers and Sisters from other Mothers".

The supreme compliment is when someone
refers to you as a
True Friend.

True Friends always make you feel as important   to
them as they are to you…
True Friends love you even when your ideas and opin-
ions are very different from theirs.

One of the many cool things about growing up in the
Bronx
was that all my closest Friends lived within
walking distance
from our Family's apartment.

PARENTING
and
KIDS
(From the perspective of a Father
and Retired Pediatrician)

When you educate your child(ren)…
You get a great opportunity to
educate or re-educate yourself.

The hardest part about disciplining a young child
is keeping a straight face.

For Football fans…
Having a second or third child
means changing the Defensive scheme
from Man-to-Man coverage to
Zone Coverage.

The two things I like and admire
most about young children
are their Honesty and their Joy for Life.

One of the most damaging things
a parent can do to their child
is underestimate their capabilities and potential.
Overestimating isn't great either,
because it places unreachable expectations
on them.

When you have difficulty understanding your child,
the answer likely lies in a full-length mirror
or in the bed next to you at night.

Parenting a Teenager is difficult,
but accepting the Truth
is far better than being an Ostrich.

When you are young and different,
people refer to you as weird.
When you grow up and are successful
but with the same traits,
you are labeled eccentric.

EMOTIONS

(Beautiful Spirit-Full Life)

The greatest gift you can give
another human being is
Unconditional Love.

A bond of Love cannot be broken,
even if you stop liking someone
for a short period of time during the relationship.

Appreciation and Loyalty top the list when looking for qualities in a potential Soul Mate.

Anger is an emotion that covers over
more painful emotions
like the outer peel of an Onion that also serves
as a protective cover.
The inner layers may contain
Hurt, Disappointment, Self-Esteem issues,
which are much harder to deal with.

Heartbreak over a broken relationship
can lead to
greater passion and intimacy in the future,
but only if one endures the pain without Anger, Bit-
terness and Resistance and moves forward slowly.

Forgiveness...
One should never forgive oneself
until forgiving others for their perceived
transgressions toward you.

True Love is
sharing intimate thoughts without speaking…
True Love is
simultaneously doing something for each other without
realizing it…
True Love is
when no compromise is too great…
True Love is
knowing Life will never be the same without her…
True Love is
when the reality far exceeds the fantasies
and the dreams.

(Dedicated to Annette)

True Courage
is creating a beautiful, meaningful life
after discovering at the age of 20 that your entire family has perished.

(Dedicated to my Father)

TRAVEL

(Half-Moon Serenity)

For those who cannot afford Foreign Travel,
don't forget about the beauty of
the Smokies, Rockies, Grand Tetons, Utah Big Five,
Grand Canyon, Glacier National Park, California,
Alaska, and Hawaii.

For some, there is the excitement of big cities like New York, Chicago, Miami, Las Vegas and New Orleans. A trip to the New Orleans Jazz and Heritage Festival in the Spring should be on everyone's bucket list.

Speaking of New Orleans,
a street musician dressed like an Alien from outer space
told me he taught himself to play the Saxophone. He
mastered the F-Flat note first, which he said was the
hardest, and the rest came easy.
Sounds like great advice for life in general.

When traveling to a Non-English speaking country,
learning a few words in the native language
can greatly enhance the quality of the trip.
Hello, Goodbye, Excuse Me, Please and Thank You
will go a long way.
In the open markets,
"How Much Does That Cost?" and
"That's Too Much" will also be helpful (LOL).

I love the sense of humor of the ancient Vikings
(not the Minnesota ones).
After exploration, they named the beautiful, lush island
with great fishing Iceland
and the more barren, frigid island Greenland.

It still fools people 1100 years later.

Whenever I think about living somewhere else
that may be more exciting or beautiful,
I remember it's not where you live,
but how you live.

LIFE

(Creative Enlightenment)

Spend your Life creating your Legacy.

Good Karma is the result
of a Life
lived unselfishly.

Life is a
series of events
beyond our control...
No scripts or scenarios
of how we want things to be.

You are either a Participant
or an Observer,
with little room in between.

Enjoy all the moments of your Life,
No need to pick or choose selectively.

A Life without Music is likely a Life without Joy.

Every second there is someone you can think about
who will bring a smile to your face.

In a good relationship,
it's wise to not hit below the belt
or bring up old stuff.

RANDOM
THOUGHTS

One thing ALL Guys have in common
(me included)
is that we all are BIG BABIES…
The biggest babies are of course
the guys who deny it.

When people say they don't
have the time to do something,
they are likely saying they wasted their time
doing something else.

As in a well-played game of Chess,
A pre-emptive Assertive move
may be necessary to go forward.

JUMPS TO TAKE

On a Trampoline
or in a game of Basketball.
In pay grade for a Job well done.
"Jump Up" at a Carnival in the West Indies.

JUMPS TO AVOID

To conclusions without gathering all the facts.
Over another person for financial gain,
undeserved recognition, and promotions.

If you believe you have attained all your Goals,
It is time to set new ones.

Every morning you wake up,
Simply be thankful for another
Day on Earth.

Single thoughts or ideas can be expressed
in just a few words
or in complicated paragraphs or long stories.

A person who tries to hide their thoughts
will usually reveal them through their actions.

If you need group approval
to validate your thought or opinion,
Its value may be questionable.

If you have to explain your intentions or actions, you might be talking to the wrong person, or the right person at the wrong time.

You are better off sharing a secret
with an understanding group
than with one person who misinterprets it.

In the Age of Technology,
a personal Hello, strong Hug and I love you
is infinitely more valuable than
all the texts, E-mails, Facebook messages, and phone
calls combined.

It may not be the easiest,
most profitable,
most convenient,
or most popular…
but it is most important to
Do the Right Thing.

"I guess I am sorry"
is not my idea of a real heartfelt apology.

It's better to enjoy and appreciate
a person's uniqueness,
than to judge and analyze it.

If you do not value the religious beliefs of others, then you devalue your own.

Everyone should be able
to laugh at themselves sometimes
and not take themselves too seriously.

They say you can learn something
from everyone you meet.
That must apply to Animals as well.
I learned the most about Unconditional Love,
Loyalty, Protectiveness, and even Grief
from our wonderful dogs and our cat Garfield.

Wisdom and Advice is best evaluated
by the quality of the message, not the messenger.
A stranger in the supermarket may impart
greater wisdom
than a Family member, friend or even your Doctor.

Happiness is a morning bike ride in the country and
being able to distinguish the difference in sounds
among Hawks, Owls, Sand Hill Cranes,
and Pileated Wood Peckers
without looking up.

Happiness is seeing the Winter Constellations
and the four brightest stars at night.
After locating Orion's Belt,
locate the third and fourth brightest stars Riegel and
Betelgeuse on either end of the Constellation.
Next, move on to the
pentagonal Auriga Constellation with the second
brightest star, Capella.
Finally, move on to the Canis Major Constellation
which resembles a tripod, and contains Sirius,
the brightest star.
Anything brighter is most likely Venus,
or possibly Mars, Saturn or Jupiter.

Every person should be entitled to die with dignity.

(Dedicated to the members of my Family who perished
in the Holocaust…)

WISDOM
Of
OTHERS

"The World is not going to change for you…
You have to change to fit into the World"
-Jakob Henry Fuchs

"You always have to be your own best friend. When you close your eyes at night, you are all you have"
-Lili Friedman Fuchs

"Love many,
Trust few,
Always paddle your own canoe"
-Helen Neumann

"Some thoughts you can share with anyone,
Some thoughts you can share with those close to you,
Some thoughts you should keep
to yourself"
-Harvey G.

"Grudge holders do more damage to themselves than to the people they begrudge"
-David T.

"There are three sides to every story"
-John M.

After you retire, "Every Day is Saturday"
-John B.

"Live every day like it's your Birthday"
-Unknown

SPECIAL ACKNOWLEDGMENTS

When I needed a transcriber to type and email my amateurish printing, I picked the perfect person. She corrected my grammar and wrong prepositions and successfully encouraged me to drop a few lame quotes. So a special shout out of thanks and appreciation to my beautiful wife, Annette, for the finishing touches.

.